A SHORT HISTORY OF

LAMBETH PALACE

Mary Cryer

Robert Cantuar

Lambeth Palace has been the London home of archbishops of Canterbury since 1197. During the week when the Archbishop is in London dealing with Church and National matters, his personal standard flies from the flagpole at the top of Lollards' Tower. At weekends, however, he returns to Canterbury, where he undertakes the normal duties of a diocesan bishop from the Old Palace, which is next door to the Cathedral. These two properties are the official residences of the Archbishop of Canterbury in the 20th century.

INTRODUCTION

ACCORDING to the *Survey of London 1951* the first reference to Lambeth has been found in the *Anglo Saxon Chronicle* of 1042 where there is the statement:

> 'This year died King Hardacnute at Lambeth as he stood drinking: he fell suddenly to the earth with a tremendous struggle; but those who were nigh at hand took him up; and he spoke not a word afterwards, but expired on the sixth day before the ides of June.'

Tradition says that he died at Kennington, but as this does not seem to have been a royal manor at the time, whereas Lambeth was, he is much more likely to have been at the latter.

From the *Domesday Book* comes this reference:

> 'St. Mary is a manor which is called *Lanchei*. Countess Goda, sister of King Edward [the Confessor] held it. It was then assessed for 10 hides; now for 2½ hides. The land is for 12 ploughs. In demesne there are 2 ploughs; and 12 villeins and 27 bordars with 4 ploughs. There is a church; and 19 burgesses in London who render 36 shillings; and there are 3 serfs; and 16 acres of meadow. Wood worth 3 hogs. In the time of King Edward and afterwards, it was worth 10 pounds; now 11 pounds.'

Goda is supposed to have given the manor of Lambeth to the church after her second marriage, and certainly it came into the possession of the Convent of St. Andrew at Rochester. The monks farmed the land and looked after the church of St. Mary until 1197 when the Manor of Lambeth was granted to Hubert Walter, Archbishop of Canterbury, in exchange for the Manor of Darenth in Kent.

When St. Augustine arrived in England in 597 to become the first in the long line of Archbishops of Canterbury, he was given a dwelling house and two churches in Canterbury by King Ethelbert of Kent as a sign of good intent. One of these churches was to become the great Cathedral that we know today.

In the earliest days the Cathedral was run by the Prior and monks of Christ Church Convent, but the Archbishop was its Abbot. Initially archbishops came from a monastic background, and many of them are regarded as saints and holy men, St. Dunstan, St. Alphege and St. Anselm among them, but by reason of their high office they were increasingly involved in national matters and became advisers to the King, even ruling in his absence. By contrast with their wider vision, the monks at Christ Church appeared insular, and the relationship between them and the archbishop was often strained. Not only that, but the monastery owed its prime allegiance to the Pope in Rome, and the Prior's independent ways – and the lavish life-style of the monks – annoyed successive archbishops.

Over the years much property and land was acquired by the archbishopric all over Kent, so wherever the Archbishop and his large retinue progressed round the diocese he could stay in his own house. But he had no London home, and by the 12th century it was becoming imperative that he should be near the King's Court when it was at Whitehall.

Dunstan, and successive archbishops, sought to be rid of the interference of the meddlesome Prior and monks at Canterbury, but it was Baldwin who obtained permission from the Pope to build a new church, a College of Secular priests at Hackington, on the outskirts of Canterbury. The intention was to dedicate this church to St. Thomas Becket. This alarmed the monks. Not only did they feel that the income from pilgrimages to the shrine would be affected, but they were quite sure that the Archbishop would seek to transfer to his new foundation the right of electing archbishops of Canterbury which hitherto they had enjoyed. The Prior appealed with success to the Pope, and the Hackington project had to be abandoned.

Baldwin was furious at the Pope's ruling, and the King was behind him. For eighty-two weeks he held the monastery in a state of siege with no supplies being allowed in, apart from what was smuggled in by friends or pilgrims visiting the shrine. Eventually the Prior and a few monks left England, without permission, and travelled to Rome to complain of their treatment, but they caught the plague that was prevalent and died. Much to the annoyance of the remaining monks, Baldwin chose a new Prior whom they did not like.

Peace was restored by form of a compromise. It was agreed that the building at Hackington should be destroyed and the new Prior deposed, but in exchange the monks would concede that the Archbishop had a right to build a collegiate church wherever he wished. He had his eye on some land owned by the See of Rochester at Lambeth, and

Left – A classical temple stands on the Temple Mound with the rear view of the Palace behind. The garden has many fine trees, many of which survived the hurricane in 1987.

by exchanging a manor at Darenth in Kent acquired this site. The Deeds of the exchange of land are held in Lambeth Palace Library. All the stone, timber and other building materials were transported by water and the new college was to begin. Baldwin was to join the King on Crusade, and died in Acre, and was succeeded by Hubert Walter.

Walter was a great builder. He brought with him his workmen who had completed his cathedral at Salisbury and enlarged the Palace at Canterbury. He ordered work to be resumed at Lambeth, but despite the assurances to the monks that they would not lose their privileges, they appealed once again to the Pope and obtained a Bull ordering the new foundation to be demolished. Walter pleaded in vain, and the building had to be pulled down. But from that time onwards the land at Lambeth and the Manor House became the official London residence of the Archbishop of Canterbury.

Walter began to build the Chapel at Lambeth but it was Stephan Langton who was the first archbishop that actually lived here. Much building was done at this time. Not all the archbishops liked living at Lambeth. The river and the marsh land bred mosquitos and malaria, and some built houses and palaces in the countryside, which suited them better. Bourchier, for instance, built the lovely house, Knowle near Sevenoaks, and Croydon Palace was much favoured as being in fresh country air.

At the Reformation many things changed: much land and property was forfeited. A Dean and Chapter took over from the Prior and monks at Canterbury, and the huge Palace there fell into disrepair. It was not until the end of the 19th century that Archbishop Frederick Temple was to restore part of it. Croydon Palace was replaced by another at Addington, which was very popular with archbishops up until this present century, but was finally relinquished by Archbishop Randall Davidson. Now only Canterbury and Lambeth remain.

Below – View from the Gardens. Thousands of daffodils and other spring bulbs have been planted here and in the Woodland Walk.

Morton's Tower is the view which most Londoners know of the Palace and which has hardly changed since it was built in 1486.

MORTON'S TOWER and GATE

THE first sight the visitor sees of the Palace is of the Tudor redbrick tower with its large entrance gate and smaller postern door, above which the tower rises to five stories high. There has always been a gateway here, but not always so impregnable, for at the time of the Peasants Revolt in the 14th century the mob were able to storm and breach the gate, pillage the Palace and force Archbishop Sudbury to flee to safely.

Cardinal Morton built and gave his name to the Tower in 1486. He was one of the chief advisers to Henry VII and was a lover of learning as well as a statesman. He might also be regarded as the Chancellor of the Exchequer of his day as he raised a tax to fill the Royal Exchequer which was known as Morton's Fork. In the fifteen years he was at Lambeth he filled it with men who were distinguished for their piety and learning. He lived in the Tower and the room above the gateway arch was used as an audience chamber. It has a fine mantlepiece and wooden panelling. His page, the young Sir Thomas More, joined the Archbishop's service at the age of twelve and had a room in the Tower on the same floor as the audience chamber. He must have learnt a good deal during his time serving the Cardinal.

On the ground floor near the Gatekeeper's office there is a small prison, with heavy rings fastened in the walls and a very small doorway. On a lintel over a door of a room on a higher floor Archbishop Parker's Chaplain carved his initials in the stone, and the coat of arms of Archbishop Tillotson was later painted on the wall. During the years many people have used these rooms and the Canterbury Registry used to be housed here, but today, apart from the Gatekeeper's apartments, the Tower is filled with archives dating back to the 9th century.

The Gate has always been guarded by a Porter, and today nobody may pass without an invitation or appointment, or being known to the Gatekeeper. In Matthew Parker's day rules and regulations were laid down so that care was taken over who passed through the portals, and especially to see what was being taken out afterwards! Parker also decreed that the Gatekeeper should keep the court outside and the passages within clean and tidy. During Chapel services and meal times the door was firmly locked.

It was from the Gate that the poor of the neighbourhood received the Lambeth Dole. Instigated by Archbishop Winchelsea (1294–1313) food and alms were given to the needy:

> 'Every Friday and Sunday, unto every beggar that came to the door, a loaf of bread of a fathing price.'

This was probably as big as a normal large loaf today. Four to five thousand people a year benefited from this and it cost the Archbishop £500 at that time. But 'Over and above this, he used to give, every great festival day, one hundred and fifty pence to so many poor people – to send daily meat, drink and bread unto such as by reason of age or sickness were not able to fetch alms at the gate.' (Godwin's, *De Praesulibus Angliae Commentarius*)

Archbishop Parker was anxious that the barrels which contained the food for the dole should 'be kept sweet and clean', and by 1806 Archbishop Manners-Sutton was providing fifteen quartern loaves, nine stone of beef and five shillings worth of half pence, which was divided into three equal portions and distributed every Sunday, Tuesday and Thursday among thirty poor parishioners in rotation. It must have been a blow to many poor families when the custom was ceased in Archbishop Howley's day and money was distributed instead. Owing to inflation in recent years the practice of giving this Corody money was discontinued after the war.

Outside the Gate and in the corner between the Tower and the Church, the sad figure of Mary of Modena, the wife of James II, sheltered on a wintry December night in 1688 when she was fleeing from London with her little son, who was to become the Young Pretender. She had crossed from Westminster in a small ferry-boat and expected to find a coach awaiting her on the Lambeth shore to transport her to the coast and from there to join her husband who was already in exile. But there was a hitch and she had to wait in the cold for the coach to come.

In the early days there was a horseferry which went from Lambeth Steps to Whitehall. It must have been a profitable enterprise as it was the only crossing at this point, and the archbishop had an interest in it. The ferrymen were a rough breed, and there were often arguments between them and their clients whom they kept waiting on the river bank in a chill wind. When Westminster Bridge was built the archbishop gave up some of his land for the approach road, and the ferrymen were put out of business. Today, on the other side of Lambeth Bridge, Horseferry Road commemorates the past.

Below – An 18th century painting of Morton's Tower which hangs in the State Drawing Room, showing a view before the Embankment was built.

The Great Hall with Cardinal Pole's fig tree growing beside it.

LOLLARDS' TOWER, with LAUD'S TOWER

FROM the Outer Courtyard a good view can be seen of the 17th century Tower built by Laud and the earlier Lollards' Tower beyond.

Archbishop Chichele built his tower in the years 1434/5. Kentish ragstone was brought by barge up the river and the cost of this was £278. 2s. 11¼d. It stood close to the quay at Lambeth Steps, where the barge was moored, and for this reason was called the Water Tower. On the river-side of the tower is a niche where the statue of St. Thomas Becket once stood. The watermen, the taxi drivers of their day, would doff their caps as they passed as a mark of respect to the saint, but the custom ceased when Henry VIII had the statue removed.

Laud's Tower is of red brick and was built in order that a better stairway could connect up to the rooms above: Laud liked looking out on to the river and these are the only rooms at Lambeth that do so. During the last War both these towers were damaged by incendiary bombs and for a while were uninhabitable. They have been carefully restored and now the rooms which were once used by some of the senior bishops when they were in London have been converted into five flats.

At the top of Chichele's Tower, under the turret where hangs a bell dated 1687, is a small prison, reached by a steep winding staircase. The doorway that guards it is made of massive wooden planks three inches thick and has a peep-hole through which a prisoner could be watched without being observed. Tradition has it that the followers of John Wycliff, the Lollards, were imprisoned here, though this is disputed. Certainly the prison was used in the 16th and 17th century, and names have been carved in the wooden panelling, with prayers and cries for help – even a set of dice. 'Chellam – Doctor; Thomas Bacar; John Worth; Pierre Amackkt; John Fyocke.' Richard Lovelace, the poet, is said to have been imprisoned here, and it was he who wrote the famous lines:

'Stone walls do not a prison make
Nor iron bars a cage.'

It is not a pleasant place even though the room has a fireplace and two windows. The original iron rings still remain in the walls to this day.

Through the Library Arch we move into the Inner Courtyard, where we get the first glimpse of the Palace itself. Built of Bath stone in Tudor Gothic style, it dates from 1830, when Archbishop Howley came to Lambeth.

Over the years the original manor house had

been repaired and enlarged on several occasions. The domestic quarters were inconvenient and Howley brought in the architect, Blore, to see what could be done. Apart from a ser of charming water-colours of different aspects of the building, Blore wrote a daunting report: 'I find in almost every respect Lambeth Palace to be miserably deficient: it is most desirable and proper that these deficiencies in the Palace, always necessarily occupied by so distinguished a person as the Archbishop of Canterbury should be supplied.' He advised the demolition of the earlier buildings and at a considerable cost the new Palace took its place. Sir Walter Scott approved of it and declared it to be in the best Gothic style 'with the splendour of church architecture returning again', but people today are very critical of the 19th century alterations and regret what has been lost – the medieval cloister, Pole's gallery and much else.

During the last war bombs fell on Lambeth on a number of occasions, and when Archbishop Fisher arrived the Chapel, Great Hall and Drawing Room were uninhabitable. It was doubtful whether Lambeth could be retained for the Archbishop in post-war Britain but, mindful that it is not only his home and his office, but a meeting place for many people, it was decided to retain it and the Church Commissioners took over the maintenance of the building. Restoration was started almost immediately to the Great Hall, and on October 19th, 1955, Fisher rededicated the Chapel in the presence of the Royal Family.

The Archbishop now lives in a flat on the top floor. There is a small but lively community living both inside the Palace and also in the cottages which were made out of the old dairy and laundry, and the Ecumenical Office is reached through the archway.

The memorial in the centre of the courtyard commemorates the twenty-five years that Randall Davidson spent as archbishop. He retired in 1929 after a long association with the Palace, beeause he was Chaplain to Archbishop Tait and had married Miss Edith Tait. The couple were much loved by Lambeth people.

Against the Great Hall wall there is a splendid fig tree. It is a dessert fig of the Marseilles variety and dates from Mary Tudor's time when her cousin, Archbishop Cardinal Pole, planted several of these trees. All the others have disappeared but this one flourishes.

A mounting stone still stands to the right of the front door, bearing witness to the days when there was a stable full of horses, and archbishops could ride to Kennington and Dulwich across open fields.

Above – The prison at the top of Lollards' Tower with iron rings in the panelled walls.

Opposite page – Lollards' Tower from the main road, with the niche which once housed the statue of Thomas Becket.

Below – 11th century Fresco of Our Lord, from northern Italy, a gift from the Pope to Archbishop Ramsey which hangs in the Chapel.

THE POST ROOM

AT the bottom of the Lollards' Tower is a fine room built by Archbishop Chichele and used as his audience chamber. The splendid early English doorway into the Chapel, which dates from Stephan Langton's time, was then the outside door of the Chapel. Above it is Laud's coat-of-arms as he did so much restoration to the Chapel in his day.

The ceiling contains some interesting carvings of angels, demi-angels and womens heads, and was supported by a big wooden post until the restoration work after the last war, when there was found to be wood-worm. It is from this post that the room gets its name. Today the Palace post box is found on the wall facing the river, and all the daily mail goes through it, and it is collected by special arrangement with the Post Office.

An old archway with double doors leads to the winding staircase to the top of the tower and the prison. Behind the stone table tomb commemorating Archbishop Parker is another doorway, now sealed up, which led down to the chamber which today houses the central-heating boiler. It is from this part of the Tower that access was obtained to the steps down to the Archbishop's barge moored on the river.

THE GREAT HALL and HOSPITALITY

THERE has been a Great Hall on this site from earliest days and it was here that in the Middle Ages the archbishop received his distinguished guests, held great councils and entertained lavishly. After the service of Consecration of a new bishop in the Chapel, a banquet would be held here at which the new bishop would sit at the head of the table wearing his mitre, whilst the archbishop and other bishops would sit with their heads uncovered. Probably the most famous and splendid of these banquets was that held in 1367 when William of Wykeham, the founder of both Winchester College and New College, Oxford, was consecrated Bishop of Winchester.

Warham entertained Erasmus and Holbein, Dean Colet and Linacre, and although Cranmer was accused by his enemies of not offering enough hospitality, his traducers had to admit to the King that a table 'as befitted the dignity of the Archbishop of Canterbury' was kept on the occasion that Henry VIII set a trap for them. Tradition tells of weekly banquets to which any gentleman could attend, providing he was properly attired in Court dress and had sent his name in previously. Three tables were set out: the first for the archbishop, nobility and gentlemen of quality; the second for bishops, abbots, clergy and the archbishop's chaplain, and the third for the steward and lesser gentry.

Large numbers of servants were kept. Cranmer had sixty, and when Cardinal Pole came from France to take his place, his cousin, Queen Mary, gave him permission to have a retinue of a hundred. By contrast Matthew Parker was very modest: although he provided a good table for guests, he himself ate simply.

In 1543 the Hall was the scene of the Special Commission, presided over by Cranmer, at which the London clergy came to take the Oath of Supremacy. Sir Thomas More was the only layman invited to it, and he and John Fisher, Bishop of Rochester, refused to take the oath, thereby sealing their fate.

During the eleven years of the Commonwealth period there was no Archbishop of Canterbury appointed after Laud's death on the scaffold. Lambeth fell into the hands of one of the regicides, Colonel Scott, who lived here and used it as a garrison and a prison for several political prisoners. He pulled down the Great Hall and auctioned off the stone. At the Restoration, Bishop Juxon of London was appointed Archbishop at the ripe old age of 78. Lambeth was handed back to him and he found the Great Hall to be 'a heap of ruins' which he was determined to restore to its former glory. He was advised that the classical style was more in keeping with the times, but he was adamant and left a sum of money in his will for the work to be completed as he wished. It must have caused considerable comment in London, and Pepys records in his diary that 'Juxon's new old-fashioned hall' was proceeding apace. It was finished in 1663, after Juxon's death, and bears witness to its builder with the coat-of-arms over the doorway and up in the roof too. Blackamoors' heads appear in Juxon's coat-of-arms, and two of them stand high over either side of the fireplace and also again in the roof. Today we are justly proud of such a good example of a mediaeval hall.

Although the Hall is mainly Gothic with its buttresses and window shapes, it has concessions to the style of the period with the hexagonal lantern which stands in the centre of the hammerbeam roof.

On the outside of this is a fine weathervane with Juxon's coat-of-arms surmounted on top in the form of a mitre. The broad doorway is of the period, as is the decoration of the cornice with its frieze of garlands and foliage. The windows show the remains of what heraldic stained glass survived the bombing during the last war.

Up until 1829 this was an open hall, but when Blore did the alterations to the Palace he brought down the Library from the gallery above. During the air-raids incendiaries fell through the roof and many books were damaged from fire and water.

In the restoration work after the war it was decided not to replace the protruding library shelves so as to allow more room in the Hall for receptions, lectures, conferences and concerts. What were the old kitchens were converted at that time into Library offices and a Reading Room. However, the Great Hall is no longer large enough to hold the large number of bishops who assemble every ten years from all parts of the Anglican Communion. Although still called the Lambeth Conference, it now takes place at The University of Kent at Canterbury.

The Leather gloves worn by Charles I to his execution in Whitehall are displayed in a glass frame. They are of soft leather and beautifully embroidered. His Chaplain, Juxon, was by his side and was handed these gloves before the King met his end. There is also a fine bust of Fisher by Epstein.

Around the room are a set of heavy dining room tables, on some of which are display cases for exhibitions which change frequently. One of these tables bears scars from the incendiaries which fell during the air-raids and which has not been restored as a reminder of that difficult time.

Above – An old engraving of the Great Hall before the restoration in 1830.

Left – Juxon's coat-of-arms contained four blackamoors' heads. This is one of them which stands over the fireplace.

Below – The fine hammer-beamed roof and lantern in the Great Hall.

THE CRYPT

THE Crypt or Undercroft, is the oldest part of Lambeth Palace and the least restored, and has been described by an archaeologist as 'the least spoiled medieval room in London'. It consists of four double bays with a central row of low Purbeck marble columns, with moulded capitals which carry chamfered arches and ribs, very similar in design to Salisbury Cathedral. This is not surprising because Hubert Walter was Bishop of Salisbury before he became Archbishop of Canterbury in 1197, and his Chief of Works, Ilias Dereham, must have come with him. We know that he was working at the same time at Southwark in the church which is now Southwark Cathedral.

Very possibly it was used as a Chapel during the rebuilding of the Chapel above in Stephen Langton's time, and over the years it has served many purposes, as a store room, wine cellar and a committee room during the 1920 Lambeth Conference. Traditionally the setting for the invalidation of Henry VIII's marriage to Anne Boleyn on May 17th, 1536, it has a door leading out to the old cloister area, and a later door with steps up to the new part of the Palace. A third door has been bricked-up.

The walls show evidence of ancient wall paintings to simulate the effect of stone. Also there is a distinct mark about four feet high where once silt covered the floor when the Thames used to flood. Archbishop Davidson had this removed in 1907 in time for the Crypt to be used as an air raid shelter during the First World War, and again in the Second.

Recently the Crypt has been cleaned and set up as a private chapel for use during the restoration of the big chapel above. There is a wonderful sense of peace and tranquility in this lovely place.

THE GUARD ROOM

THE Guard Room dates from the 14th century and has a splendid arched-braced roof of the wagon type, which is supported on corbels and has tracery in the spandrels, making it one of the finest roofs in the country.

At its name implies, it was originally used by the men-at-arms which the Archbishop employed, as did other princes and great lords of the Middle Ages. There is no doubt that this was necessary in those turbulent times. Indeed in 1381, Archbishop Sudbury was forced to flee from Lambeth when the mob broke in through the gate and much damage was done. By the 15th century the room was transformed into the armoury with coats-of-arms and weapons of all kinds. Pikes from this period were discovered buried in the garden, and are now displayed at the top of the Main Staircase.

By the 18th century the Guard Room became a dining room and it has been used as such many times since then. It is a very useful room in the present day because it can serve so many purposes: a conference room, a concert hall for chamber music and a reception room for numbers up to 200. There are dinner parties held here when the numbers are too great for the Blue Dining Room to hold, and many charitable appeals have been launched from this room.

The room was restored at the time of the rebuilding in 1829 when the roof was preserved intact as it was propped up until the new walls were ready to receive it. It was again restored after the bombing of the Second World War.

It was in this room that Thomas More is believed to have faced examination by the Lords of the Council following his refusal to take the Oath of Supremacy in 1534, and where in 1867 seventy-five bishops – not all of whom were pleased to have been summoned from their dioceses – met for the first Lambeth Conference presided over by Archbishop Longley. The Conference has now become a regular ten-yearly event, broken only during the period of the wars, and as so many bishops from overseas attend it, Lambeth is no longer able to accommodate the numbers.

Above – The Guard Room, where the portraits of the 17th and 18th century archbishops hang.

Left – The Crypt, in use as a private chapel.

Around the walls look down portraits of the 17th and 18th century archbishops, painted by the leading portrait painters of the day, Lely, Dance, Hogarth, Kneller, Sir Joshua Reynolds and romney, and they show how the fashion in ecclesiastical dress has changed over the years. The Canterbury caps of the 17th century are replaced by the wigs of the 18th century, and ruffs are replaced by bands, whilst the sleeves become fuller and fuller.

The picture of Archbishop Laud, attributed to Van Dyke, hung in the Archbishop's study in his day. An entry in his diary in October 1640 records that upon returning to his room he found the picture lying on the floor, as the cord by which it hung had broken. 'God grant that this be no omen!', the superstitious Archbishop noted. A few weeks later the soldiers came to take him prisoner, and he remained at the Tower of London until his execution on Tower Hill.

Two examples of the corbels in the Guard Room.

Some prominent archbishops

Henry Chichele

Thomas Cranmer

Reginald Pole

Matthew Parker

William Laud

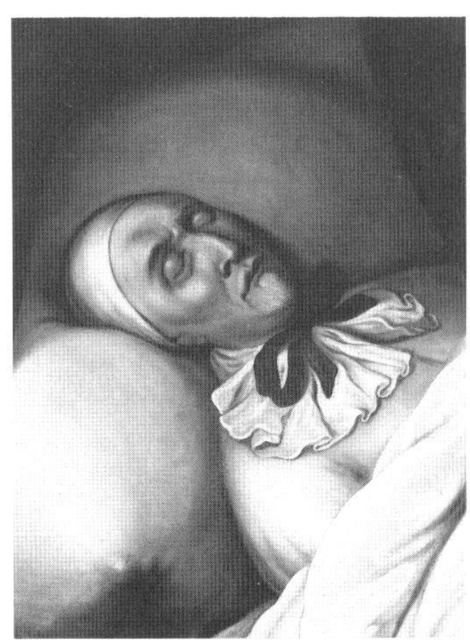

William Juxon

Charles Longley

Randall Davidson

William Temple

Michael Ramsey

Donald Coggan

Robert Runcie

LIST OF ARCHBISHOPS OF CANTERBURY

In some cases dates assigned are only approximate

597 Augustine
604 Laurentius
619 Mellitus
624 Justus
627 Honorius
655 Deusdedit
668 Theodorus
693 Beorhtweald
731 Tatwine
735 Nothelm
740 Cuthbeorht
761 Breguwine
765 Jaenbeorht
793 Æthelheard
805 Wulfred
832 Feologild
833 Ceolnoth
870 Æthelred
890 Plegmund
914 Æthelhelm
923 Wulfhelm
942 Oda
959 Æfsige
959 Beorhthelm
960 Dunstan
988 Athelgar
990 Sigeric Serio
995 Ælfric
1005 Ælfheah
1013 Lyfing
1020 Æthelnoth
1038 Eadsige
1051 Robert of Jumieges
1052 Stigand
1070 Lanfranc
1093 Anselm
1114 Ralph d'Escures
1123 William Corbeil
1139 Theobald
1162 Thomas Becket
1174 Richard of Dover
1185 Baldwin
1193 Hubert Walter
1207 Stephen Langton
1229 Richard le Grant
1234 Edmund of Abingdon
1245 Boniface of Savoy
1273 Robert Kilwardby
1279 John Pecham
1294 Robert Winchelsey
1313 Walter Reynolds
1328 Simon Meopham
1333 John Stratford
1349 Thomas Bradwardine
1349 Simon Islip
1366 Simon Langham
1368 William Whittlesey
1375 Simon Sudbury
1381 William Courtenay
1396 Thomas Arundel
1398 Roger Walden
1399 Thomas Arundel (Restored)
1414 Henry Chichele
1443 John Stafford
1452 John Kempe
1454 Thomas Bourchier
1486 John Morton
1501 Henry Deane
1503 William Warham
1533 Thomas Cranmer
1556 Reginald Pole
1559 Matthew Parker
1576 Edmund Grindal
1583 John Whitgift
1604 Richard Bancroft
1611 George Abbot
1633 William Laud
1660 William Juxon
1663 Gilbert Sheldon
1678 William Sancroft
1691 John Tillotson
1695 Thomas Tenison
1716 William Wake
1737 John Potter
1747 Thomas Herring
1757 Matthew Hutton
1758 Thomas Secker
1768 Frederick Cornwallis
1783 John Moore
1805 Charles Manners-Sutton
1828 William Howley
1848 John Bird Sumner
1862 Charles Thomas Longley
1868 Archibald Campbell Tait
1883 Edward White Benson
1896 Frederick Temple
1903 Randall Thomas Davidson
1928 Cosmo Gordon Lang
1942 William Temple
1945 Geoffrey Francis Fisher
1961 Arthur Michael Ramsey
1974 Frederick Donald Coggan
1980 Robert Alexander Kennedy Runcie

THE CHAPEL

A Chapel was in existence from the early days of the 13th century and one of the earliest of the Court of Account Rolls at Lambeth, that for 1234, speaks of a payment to a glazier for the repair of the Chapel windows.

By 1243 repairs were necessary to the building to celebrate the arrival of Boniface of Savoy as Archbishop. Later a fine pair of windows were put in during Morton's time, and Archbishop Laud spent much money and care on his redecorations. The altar rail dates from this time, as do some of the pews and the bench ends and the fine oak screen. Laud was accused of Popish sympathies by Prynne because he repaired Laud's windows, and you will notice at the foot of the windows behind the Altar there are three dates: 1496 – when Morton's windows were installed; 1634 – when Laud repaired them; and then 1955 when the new windows were put in after the last war. These new windows record the same subjects as the earlier windows and were made by the artists Carl Edwards and Hugh Powell, preserving the same tradition and continuity throughout.

Much damage was done during the Commonwealth, when the Chapel was used as a drinking room for the soldiers. They destroyed the stained glass windows, and broke up Archbishop Parker's tomb, throwing out his embalmed body. It is recorded in Dart's *Antiquities of Canterbury*, 1806, 'Tomb dug up by Hardynge to whose share this part of the Palace fell, opening the leaden coffin and cut away the cerecloths of which there were many foldes, the flesh seemed very fresh. The corpse thus stripped was conveyed into the outhouse for poultry and dung, and buried amongst the offal, but upon the restoration of King Charles II that wretch Hardynge was forced to discover where it was, whereupon the Archbishop had him honourably re-interred in the same chapel.' In fact the spot was marked with an inscribed stone in the

floor, and would have been the place where Parker knelt for the laying-on-of-hands at his consecration.

In Howley's rebuilding and redecoration the Chapel roof reverted from the flat roof of Laud's day to a lofty vaulted roof, similar to the original one. The walls were lavishly painted and new stained glass windows were put in. All this was lost during the 1939–45 war, when bombs fell and demolished the roof and the stained glass. The screen and woodwork was removed and tarpaulins covered the damage until work began to restore it.

In 1955 a service of re-dedication took place with Archbishop Fisher officiating in the presence of Her Majesty the Queen and other members of the Royal Family. The work was dignified but was completed in a period of austerity and it was felt that much of the history and mystery of the older chapel was lost. For that reason the Chapel has again been restored: the screen replaced in its original position, and the ceiling painted by Mr. Leonard Rosoman, R.A., depicting historical scenes, the stalls restored to their original position and twenty-five of them named for the equal number of Anglican Primates who meet regularly under the chairmanship of the Archbishop of Canterbury.

The removal of some stalls has revealed a quantity of mediaeval tiles which were part of the flooring prior to Laud's restoration. This has occasioned great interest, especially one area which is laid in the original chevron pattern. Dating is difficult, but similar tiles can be found in Southwark and Westminster, and there are nineteen different designs ranging from hunting scenes to the three lions in the Arms of Kings of England in a form used up to 1340, which make the Lambeth tiles a valuable collection. They remain in situ, but can be displayed.

Left – After Laud's restoration, showing the flat roof and wooden panelling which was a feature of the Chapel of his day.

Below – A section of the mediaeval tiles unearthed during the current restoration of the Chapel.

Left – Mr. Leonard Rosoman, R.A., during the painting of the Chapel ceiling, which brings back much of the history of Lambeth.

Far right – A Chapel bench head dating from Laud's restoration during the 1640's.

Below – One of the Chapel ceiling paintings: The Consecration of Matthew Parker, which took place in 1559 in the Chapel.

Below right – Another of the ceiling paintings: Pope Gregory commissioning Augustine to bring the faith to England.

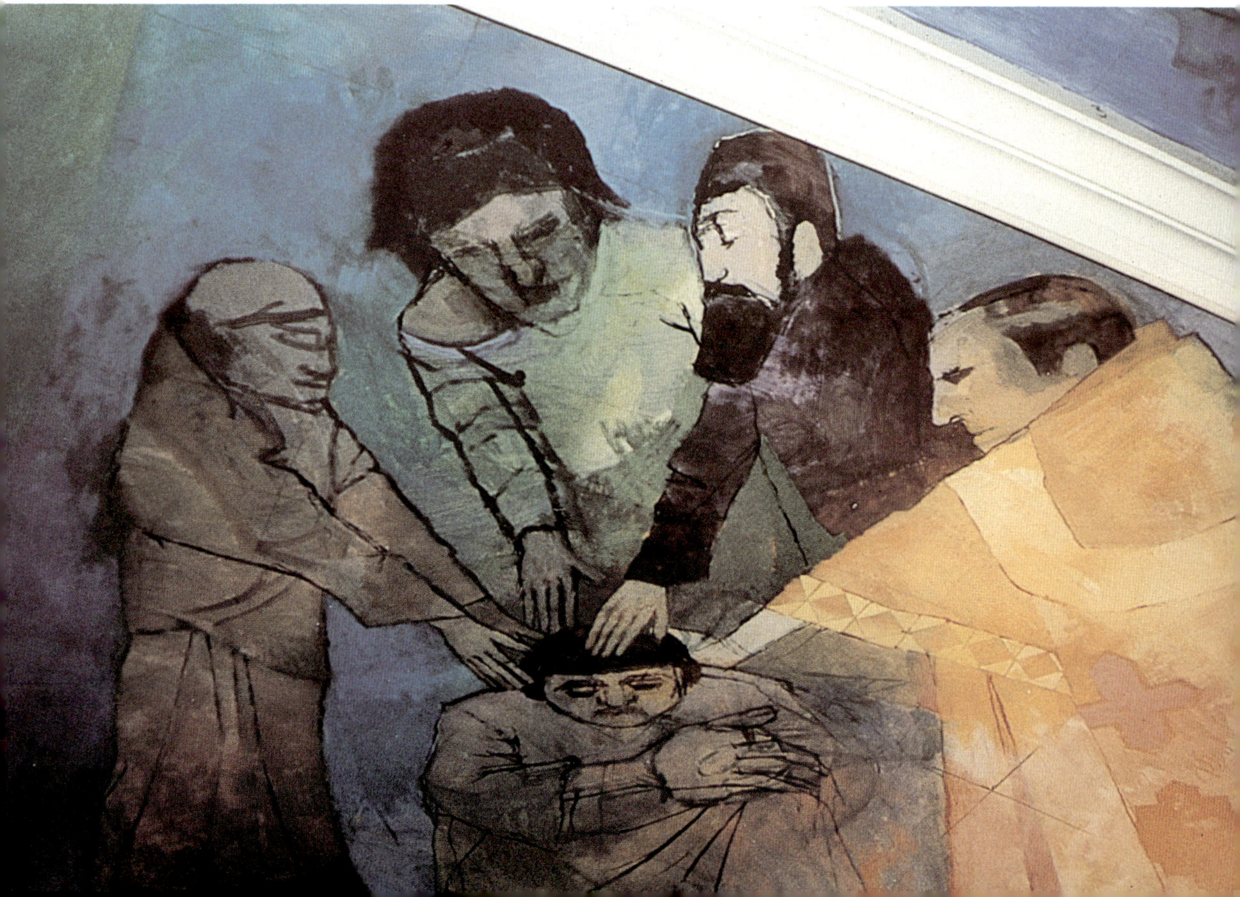

The Chapel has seen much history pass through it. It was here that Wycliff was tried in 1378; here that Matthew Parker was consecrated in a service of great significance for the continuity of the Anglican Church; here that Laud was praying when the soldiers came to arrest him in 1640; here where nearly all the bishops were consecrated up to the 1870's, and where overseas bishops and missionaries were consecrated for work abroad. In 1787 William White was consecrated Bishop of Pennsylvania, Samuel Provost, Bishop of New York, and then three years later, James Madison was consecrated Bishop of Virginia. In 1872 in recognition of this link a present of a gold alms dish was presented from 'The New World to the Old, the West to the East, the Daughter to the Mother'.

To the left of the High Altar, windows can be seen which lead into Cranmer's Parlour, a panelled room similar to the Vestry below, where Cranmer worked on the Prayer Book. The room now houses the collection of books and pamphlets left to Lambeth by Bishop J. A. T. Robinson.

The stained glass windows were the work of the artists Carl Edwards and Hugh Powell after the war, and are in the same tradition and continuity of the windows that Morton first installed in 1486.

THE LIBRARY

THE Library was founded in 1610 by Archbishop Bancroft. Earlier Archbishops had their own private libraries and there are books here which bear Cranmer's name on the fly-leaf and Whitgift's coat-of-arms. In his will Bancroft left all his books to Lambeth . . . 'I give all my books in my study over the cloisters unto my successors and to the archbishops of Canterbury successively for ever'. Abbot added to the collection and although Laud's books were divided on his death between the University of Cambridge and St. John's College, Oxford, Juxon was able to recover those at Cambridge for the Lambeth Collection. Those at St. John's College remain to this day.

Down the ages books and papers have been added, and are still added, by the generosity of the Friends of Lambeth Palace Library. Although at one time it was the first free public library in London, today the collection is one of the principal libraries in the country for historical and other studies. Registers, Court Rolls and Charters go back to the 13th century and one of the treasures is the last Will and Testament of Dick Whittington, Lord Mayor of London.

Part of the collection are illuminated manuscripts and bibles, including the famous Lambeth Bible, dating from the 11th century which was written at Canterbury, and the MacDurnan Gospels written in the 9th century. There is a wonderful 11th century Apocalypse – possibly the work of the monks at St. Augustine's Abbey, Canterbury, and an Atlas made by Battisto Agnese in the 16th

century. A recent addition has been a 15th century manuscript from Italy of Leonardo Fescobaldi's narrative of a pilgrimage to the Holy Land in 1384.

Among the rare printed books is the New Testament, part of the first bible to be printed with moveable metal type at Mainz in the 1450's, known as the *Gutenburg Bible*. This copy is printed on vellum with illuminations by hand. There is a manuscript copy of Caxton's *Chronicles of England*, and the book known as *The Prayers of the Lady Margaret*, mother of Henry VII, probably the work of Wynkyn de Worde. There are early editions of works by Erasmus. Wycliffe and Luther.

Apart from ecclesiastical subjects such as church histories, books of sermons, psalters and missals, there are interesting collections of papers, such as the Talbot papers, which show life in Tudor times, and the Earl of Essex's papers when, in addition to being Elizabeth I's favourite, he was also in touch with the Continent on all matters of the day. There are eye-witness accounts such as the divorce of Katharine of Aragon, the death of Queen Elizabeth, the capture of Cadiz, parliamentary procedure before *Hansard* came to record it, and the diaries of Lord Gladstone.

There is an annual meeting to which Friends are invited, after which a lecture is given. To become a Friend application is made to the Librarian direct.

Left – View of part of the Great Hall which houses the Library. A bust of Archbishop Fisher (1945) by Epstein stands here.

Below: A page from the famous Lambeth Bible relating to Ruth and Boaz. The Bible dates from the 11th century.

THE CLOISTER or PICTURE GALLERY

FROM the Library stairs running to Laud's Tower is a gallery which skirts a quiet, peaceful cloister. Until the 1828 alterations this was the site of the mediaeval cloister, which was still in good order at the time of Matthew Parker, and although this gallery is part of the new building it replaced an existing gallery where once the library would have been found.

Indeed from a window in this gallery, opposite the portrait of Archbishop Parker, Queen Elizabeth I looked down into the cloister where the Chaplain preached a Lenten sermon on the occasion of her visit to Lambeth early in her reign. The record suggests that the royal presence attracted more attention than the sermon itself! Although on good terms with her archbishop, the Queen disapproved of married clergy, and Margaret Parker was the first archbishop's wife to play an active part in the life of the Palace. When time came to depart the Queen must have enjoyed Margaret's hospitality, and she rather grudgingly said to her 'Madam I may not call you; mistress I am ashamed to call you; so I know not what to call you: yet I thank you'!

From the archives of the period we can see how busily both the Parkers entered into the life of the Palace. Margaret drew up rules for the cleanliness of the kitchens, and the herbs to be planted in the garden for cooking. She earned the nick-name 'Her Grace', whereas her husband, with his interest in all things as well as his rather large nose, was affectionately known by his colleagues as 'Nosey Parker'.

This gallery displays the earliest portraits we have of archbishops, including those who were involved with the Reformation (see chapter on

Above – The old panelled room which faces on to the Chapel, which was Cranmer's study.
Left – The Picture Gallery leading to Laud's Tower.

Portraits). There are some ancient vestments with a chevron design printed on silk which date to the time of Cardinal Pole, and a collection of miniatures of early reformers which Archbishop Sancroft left to his successors.

Archbishop Laud brought both a cat and a tortoise to Lambeth. The cat stayed for only a few days, but the tortoise remained for 120 years. Unfortunately in 1753 a gardener unwittingly overturned a wheelbarrow on top of it and killed it. He must have been severely reprimanded at the time, because a brass plaque commemorates his negligence, and the shell remains to this day in a display cabinet in the gallery.

Also on display is a pane of glass, which came from a window in the Palace at Croydon, which bears the words scratched upon it:

> 'MEMORAND: Ecclesiae de Micham, Cheme and Stone sum aliis fulgure combustae sünt. Januari 14 1638/9
>
> Omen Auertat Deus.'

These words are believed to have been inscribed by Laud himself. Obviously there was a fire-raiser at work that winter, and in my parish church at Cheam there are still signs of the fire on monuments in the Lumley Chapel, which is all that remains now of the original church.

THE DRAWING ROOMS and GREAT CORRIDOR

ON either side of the Great Corridor, where the portraits of the archbishops since 1837 hang, are the Drawing Rooms.

The Pink Drawing Room faces the Inner Courtyard and has the original decorated ceiling. Before the upstairs kitchen was built there was another window in what is now an alcove, but the room is bright and sunny. This is the quiet side of the building, where traffic noises do not penetrate.

The Dining Room and State Drawing Room were destroyed by bombs during the last war as were the rooms above. When they were rebuilt the original bay windows were not replaced, neither was the ceiling. Restored quite recently, the two rooms were decorated to match and have a splendid view of the garden. The dinner service, made for Archbishop Howley to entertain Queen Victoria, is from the Worcester factory. Green and gold on white, it is decorated with the mitre. Down the ages pieces got broken in use, and replacements were commissioned, until at last there are plates from the Ridgeway factory which are nothing like so fine as the originals.

These rooms, which were once used by archbishops as their private quarters, are now the scene of official functions and for entertaining the many visitors that come to Lambeth in the course of the year.

On this floor the Archbishop's study and secretariat take up a large area, which extends to the ground floor too. A commanding flight of stairs leads up from the front door, and at the top is a

bell marked 'Footman' which no longer works; but since Archbishop Lang's day there would be nobody to answer it, so nobody minds! The stairs are gentle ones, but there is an amusing story of the occasion when Lang entertained Lord Halifax to dinner. Always a robust man, Lang was taken ill shortly after his arrival at Lambeth, and at the time was convalescing. At the end of the evening the Archbishop escorted the old man down the stairs carefully, and half way down they slipped and both fell together in a huddle at the bottom. Fortunately neither of them was hurt and the two men were able to laugh as they picked themselves up and said farewell.

Left – The State Drawing Room, which was badly damaged during the Second World War.

Right – The Staircase, showing Blore's fondness for the Gothic in the design of the bannisters and lights.

Below – The Great Corridor where portraits of all the archbishops from Victorian times hang.

Recipes from the Archives

Dr. Burges His approved Medecine against the Plague

Take 3 pints of muscadel and boyle therein a handfull of sage and a handfull of rew, til a pint be wasted, then straine it and sett it over the fire againe, then put thereto a pennyworth of long pepper, halfe an ounce of ginger and a quarter of an ounce of nutmeggs, all beaten together, then let it boyle a little, and put thereto 2 pennyworth of treacle, 4 pennyworth of methridate and a quarter of a pint of the best hot water made with angeleco water. Take of this always warme both morning and evening a spoonfull or two, if you bee already infected; halfe a spoonfull in the morning and halfe at evening, if you bee not infected. This never failed man, woman or child.

This is not only good for the common plague but for the smallpox, measells and surgetts and divers other deseases.

Probatum est.

Two recipes from Mrs. Tenison's Recipe Book

To make Red Marmalett

Take two pounds and a halfe of sugar, then take 3 pounds of quinces and pare them very cleane, and take two pints of water and boyle the water and sugar together, and skime it very cleare, then put in your quinces and let them boyle untill they bee tender, and then you must cover them with a dish very close, and soe bate the fier and let them simper untill they come to their coloure, and now and then stirr them with your ladle, and of your owne judgement as you like the Coloure you must let them boyle up to the topp and then take them off and straine them through a Cullender and soe beat them to morter, then put them into your liquor that you strained from them and boyle them untill you thinke they will cut and then put it into boxes.

To make Cherry Marmalett

Take 2 pounds of Cherryes to 1 lb of sugar, wett your sugar with juyce of redcurrance, allow a little sugar, for the juyce or if you cannot get currance doe it with the juyce of Cherries, stone the cherryes and put all together into a skellit, set them on a quick fire and let them boyle till you thinke they are enough, then putt them in glasses.

THE GARDENS

THE grounds at Lambeth used to stretch as far as the Lambeth Marsh and flanked the river nearly up to Westminster Bridge. From the time when the monks lived here and worked the Manor land the garden has been cared for and cultivated. Herbs and fruit were planted as well as flowers in formal beds and there was a moat which divided the grazing land from the more cultivated area.

Archeologists have recently dug and found relics of Roman days and also flint tools dating back two thousand years, but so far no remains of an early settlement have been discovered.

Cranmer, Parker and Laud spent time in the garden and in the archives from Parker's time is the following instruction: 'to see the garden, orchard and walks to be kept well weeded and rolled, the grass walks not suffered to be much grown, but kept low with the scythe. To see there be planted in the grounds flowers, herbs and roots, both for the provision for the kitchen and chambers; and with all sorts of good fruits, herbs, plants and flowers for use and pleasure.'

Successive archbishops improved the garden in various ways, greenhouses built and lots of trees and shrubs planted, some of which survive even to this day. The dove cote, a summer house and Archbishop Tenison's rabbit house, which he 'erected without royal license', has long since disappeared.

The people of Lambeth had a sports day once a year in the grounds and at the end of the 19th century Archbishop Frederick Temple permitted the transfer on perpetual loan of a large field, which adjoined the more formal gardens, to the London County Council for use as a recreation ground. It is known today as Archbishop's Park.

The Gardens:
left – The herb garden;
top right – The lake;
bottom left – The woodland walk;
bottom right – The terrace.

The garden is still extensive, despite the loss of land for the approach to Westminster Bridge and the the plot on which St. Thomas' Hospital now stands, and only Buckingham Palace has bigger grounds in the centre of London. Lambeth stands on some 10½ acres today, of which the building itself takes up nearly 2 acres.

In the last war a Barrage Balloon Station was set up on the lawns and a lot of the land was cultivated for 'Dig for Victory'. When hostilities ceased it was grassed over and reverted to park land.

Recently, under the inspired supervision of Mrs. Runcie, much work has been done to restore the gardens. New trees and shrubs planted in place of old and dead wood. A herb garden, a Chinese garden, a cottage garden, and a fragrant garden have been created and at the bottom of the Woodland Walk is a wild garden flanking a small pond, all of which creates an oasis of peace in the heart of busy London.

PICTURES and PERSONALITIES

There is a fine collection of paintings at Lambeth Palace which have been acquired over the years. Painted b notable artists of their day, few are landscapes, most are portraits. Since the time of the Reformation we hav a picture of all the Archbishops of Canterbury up to the present. The dates shown are the year in which th archbishop took up office.

Most of the pictures listed here can be seen on a tour of the Palace, but those marked with an asterisk ar hanging in private rooms.

THOMAS ARUNDEL
British School
29¾ x 24¾ ins.

60th Archbishop (1396)
The first to have a portrait at Lambeth. His arms appear on left hand corner, opposite red rose of Lancaster. Impeached and exiled by Richard II, returned to his office to enthrone and crown Henry IV. Arundel was distinguished chiefly for his zeal against the Lollards, and during his day the first Englishman was burnt at the stake for heresy.

HENRY CHICHELE
British School
19½ x 16 ins.
panel

Archbishop (1414)
The founder of All Souls, Oxford, and builder of Lollards' Tower at Lambeth. His is the only picture of an archbishop wearing a mitre and giving the Blessing.

WILLIAM WARHAM
After Holbein
31 x 26 ins.

Archbishop (1503)
This picture was lost during the Commonwealth and recovered by Sir William Dugdale. For years it was thought to be a genuine Holbein.

THOMAS CRANMER
British School
1. 23 x 17½ ins. panel
2. 30 x 24½ ins.

Archbishop (1533)

Inscribed Martyr.

Inscription on the back reads: 'Property of Archbishop Benson by whom it was purchased Easter 1886.' The famous Reformation Archbishop, who died at the stake. Whilst at Lambeth he had a retinue of 60. Tradition says that he walked with Anne Boleyn in the Crypt to discuss the Royal divorce.

REGINALD POLE
Italian School
1. 21 x 18 ins. panel
2. 45 x 35 ins.

Archbishop (1556)

Latin inscription over head, other wording defaced.
Copy of one in the Barbarini Palace, Rome.
Pole was the cousin of Mary Tudor, who brought him over from France at her accession. She gave him furniture for the Palace and allowed him a retinue of 100. He is shown in both pictures wearing the robes of a cardinal, and brought with him silks, tapestries and brocades which brought colour to Lambeth. He was ill with malaria when the Queen died and outlived her by 24 hours. He was our last Roman Catholic Archbishop.

MATTHEW PARKER
1. British School 27 x 21 ins. panel
2. By Richard Lyne 14 x 10 ins. dated 1572

Archbishop (1559)
This wise and moderate primate was chosen by Elizabeth I to serve the difficult period at the beginning of h reign. His consecration took place i the Chapel here, performed by Barlo Bishop Elect of Chichester; Scory, Bishop Elect of Hereford; Coverdale Late Bishop of Exeter; and Hodgkin Suffragan Bishop of Bedford, and it through him that the Anglican Chur claimed the Apostolic succession. Although Cranmer was married, Park was the first to bring his wife into prominence at Lambeth. Archives show that Matthew and Margaret Parker ordered the life at Lambeth, to the way the kitchens and herb garden should be stocked and to the duties of the Gatekeeper. Respected and liked by his bishops, he was nicknamed 'Nosey Parker' because c his curiosity and large nose.

EDMUND GRINDAL
30 x 25 ins.
inscribed De Vos

Archbishop (1576)
Grindal soon lost the confidence of Elizabeth I because of his Calvanist sympathies. Edmund Spenser in his 'Shepherd's Calendar' celebrates Grindal under the name of 'Algrind'

JOHN WHITGIFT
British School
1. 23 x 17½ ins. inscribed '1602 Vincit qui patitur'
2. 15 x 11 ins. Holding wreath, with forefinger of left hand in book, black beard. Area painted in margin *

Archbishop (1583)
Founder of the famous school at Croydon. Very popular with Elizabet I as, like the monarch, he delighted in gorgeous ceremonies and hated the Puritans. It was he who drew up a series of articles to which he require all clergy to subscribe before ordination, affirming the Royal Supremacy, the Act of Uniformity and the Thirty-Nine Articles. He wa present at the deathbed of Elizabetl I, and crowned James I. He died of a cold caught on a journey from Lambeth to Fulham in his barge anc was struck down with paralysis.

RICHARD BANCROFT
British School
1. 22 x 17 ins.
2. 24 x 18 ins.

Archbishop (1604)
A vigorous opponent of the Puritan and zealous in asserting the divine right of episcopacy, he tried hard to improve the quality of the priesthoc We owe the Lambeth Palace Library to Bancroft who bequeathed to his successors a valuable collection of books.

EORGE ABBOT
ritish School
9½ x 24 ins.

Archbishop (1611)
Unlike his predecessors he had a strong Puritan bias though he had no favour for nonconformity. In 1621 while hunting on Lord Zouche's land in Hampshire a keeper was struck by an arrow from Abbot's cross-bow and subsequently died. Although in no way to blame as the keeper had been warned to keep out out of the way, the Archbishop was thrown into deep depression, and for the rest of his life fasted on Tuesday, the day of the accident.

ILLIAM LAUD
ttributed to
'an Dyke
0 x 40 ins.

Archbishop (1644)
A supporter of Charles I, Laud had a naturally arrogant manner which made enemies. His great friend was the Earl of Strafford, who was to be executed shortly before he himself went to the scaffold. Laud did much work to restore Lambeth Palace Chapel and built a tower so that he could have rooms overlooking the river. His portrait hung in his study and one day he entered it to find that the cord had broken and the picture was on the floor. Being superstitious he thought it a bad omen, and three weeks later he was taken by the soldiers to the Tower of London.

ILLIAM JUXON
ritish School
1. 29¾ x 24 ins. Library vestibule, inscribed 1633
2. 50 x 40 ins. After the portrait at Longleat

Archbishop (1660)
Juxon had been Chaplain to Charles I and had attended him on the scaffold. At the Restoration he was chosen to fill the vacancy that had remained since Laud's execution. Juxon repaired and restored Lambeth after the damage of the Commonwealth years, and the Great Hall was completed to his design. His coat-of-arms can be seen in the Great Hall and in the Chapel.

ILBERT SHELDON
ely
0 x 40 ins.

Archbishop (1663)
A supporter of Charles I he had been imprisoned during the Commonwealth and was rewarded with the Bishopric of London at the Restoration. He stayed at Lambeth during the Plague, exposed to great danger, and after the Fire of London gave £2000 towards the rebuilding of St. Paul's. He was made Chancellor of the University of Oxford in 1667 and the Sheldonian Theatre was erected at his own expense. He lost favour with Charles II when he rebuked his shameless adultery and refused him the sacrament. He is said to have offended the Puritans by declaring that honest deeds were of more value than pious words.

ILLIAM ANCROFT
. Lens
0 x 40 ins.

Archbishop (1677)
One of his first acts as Archbishop was to persuade the Duke of York (later James II) to renounce Catholicism and embrace the Church of England. He was to crown him later according to the usual service but without the Communion being administered. Sancroft, together with six other bishops, petitioned against the Declaration of Indulgences which was to be read out in churches, and there followed the famous trial, but all seven were found Not Guilty. On the same day as the aquittal a letter was sent to William of Orange signed by English noblemen, inviting him to come and save the religion and laws of the land. But when Sancroft realised that William wanted the Crown for himself he disassociated himself from Parliament and refused to take the oath of allegiance whilst James II was alive and in exile. For this he was deposed, and retired to his house in the country.

TRIAL OF THE SEVEN BISHOPS
British School
41 x 66 ins. *

JOHN TILLOTSON
1. Kneller
50 x 40 ins.
2. British School
Head only,
11 x 9 ins. *
3. British School
29½ x 58¼ ins. *

Archbishop (1691)
Tillotson advocated considerable latitude in matters of belief and practice. While the Prayer Book was under examination he revised the collects, making them more suitable to the epistle and gospel of the day. His portrait reveals a more modern face than his predecessors and he was known for his geniality and hospitality and was esteemed the best preacher of his day by Bishop Burnet.

THOMAS TENISON
Simon du Bois
50 x 40 ins.

Archbishop (1695)
Tenison was deeply interested in founding the Society for the Propagation of the Gospel and the first meeting of the Society took place at Lambeth. Tenison crowned both Queen Anne and George I and made an impression on the new monarch because, during a meeting of an hour and a half, he never once asked a favour for himself or his friends.

WILLIAM WAKE
I. Whood
50 x 40 ins.
signed and dated 1736

Archbishop (1716)
Wake was very interested in the Gallic Church and corresponded with Du Pin, the ecclesiastical historian, and other gallican divines with the project of union between the English and French Church. He was perhaps the first Ecumenical Archbishop, showing a deep interest in the welfare of other foreign Protestant Churches, and was in communication with the Eastern Church.

JOHN POTTER
T. Hudson
56 x 44½ ins.
signed and dated 1746

Archbishop (1737)
Although a High Churchman, Potter was a Whig in politics. During his primacy the Wesley brothers caused a great religious revival, and Potter showed much interest in the Methodist Movement: 'These gentlemen are irregular, but they have done much good, and I pray God to bless them.'

THOMAS HERRING
1. After Hogarth
   50 x 40 ins.
   dated 1747
2. Hogarth
   50 x 40 ins.

Archbishop (1747)
Before he came to Canterbury, Herring was Bishop of Bangor and then Archbishop of York. He had a pastoral heart and visited the parishes in these two dioceses making detailed notes of parochial life. He possessed a cultivated mind but it is generally supposed that he obtained promotion due to the support he gave to the House of Hanover after the rebellion of 1745. This was the time when *The Beggars Opera* was taking London by storm. Herring preached against it much to Dean Swift's disgust.

MATTHEW HUTTON
Thomas Hudson
50 x 40 ins.

Archbishop (1757)
Hutton was destined to follow Herring around from Bangor to York and finally Canterbury. He found Lambeth Palace very dilapidated due to Herring's neglect, and never moved in, preferring to use his house in Duke Street.

THOMAS SECKER
1. Joshua Reynolds
   50 x 40 ins.
   Repeat of portrait at St. Edmunds Hall
2. British School
   50 x 40 ins.
   (As Bishop of Bristol and Oxford)

Archbishop (1758)
A kindly man who suffered weak health, he graduated as a Doctor of Physic at Leydon before being ordained. He was a classical scholar and well-skilled in Hebrew and his sermons were much admired for their manly sense. However, Horace Walpole, who detested him, thought otherwise and insisted 'That they were a kind of moral essay and what they wanted of the gospel was made up by a tone of fanaticism . . .'. He was buried simply as he wished, without monument or epitaph outside the church of St. Mary, Lambeth.

FREDERICK CORNWALLIS
Dance
50 x 40 ins.

Archbishop (1768)
The first primate of high birth since the days of Cardinal Pole, Cornwallis was the seventh son of Lord Cornwallis and was a twin of General Edward Cornwallis of the American Civil War fame. His wife was a leader of society and gave large balls and routs at the Palace, which drew censure from many quarters! Cornwallis was a man of liberal views, tolerant towards dissenters and Roman Catholics. He improved Lambeth and added many pictures of his predecessors.

JOHN MOORE
1. Romney
   50 x 40 ins.
2. 'Kneller'
   Bishop Moore of Ely, 1707

Archbishop (1783)
The son of a grazier, Moore became tutor to the Duke of Marlborough's son. An accomplished man, he was a strong supporter of Sunday Schools and all missionary enterprises. In 1787 he consecrated two missionary bishops in the Chapel (for North America, and Nova Scotia). He is said to have exercised undue influence over George III during the King's periods of mental disorder.

CHARLES MANNERS-SUTTON
Sir John Lawrence
59½ x 49½ ins.

Archbishop (1805)
During his primacy there was a grea revival of life and energy within the Church of England. The archbishop threw his weight behind the orthodo High Church party whereas his immediate predecessors had support the evangelical party. Manners-Sutto improved the financial state of the Se by selling the old archiepiscopal pala at Croydon and buying a new palace at nearby Addington. His family held high positions, his brother being Chancellor of Ireland and his son Speaker of the House of Commons.

WILLIAM HOWLEY
1. Owen
   On loan from the National Portrait Gallery
2. Martin Shee
   56 x 44 ins.

Archbishop (1828)
Howley ordered the demolition of the old domestic quarters of the Palace and had the new building erected in its place. He accompanied the Lord Chamberlain in the early hours of th morning to Kensington Palace to inform the Princess Victoria of her accession to the throne. In sympathy with the founders of the Oxford Movement, he roused their indignati when he consecrated the first bishop for Jerusalem in the Chapel which seemed to them to be meddling with the jurisdiction of the Eastern Church

JOHN BIRD SUMNER
Eddis
56 x 44 ins.

Archbishop (1848)
In 1852, Convocation met for the firs time for 135 years, and eight years later Sumner had to deal with the problems raised by the publication o the controversial book *Essays and Reviews.* It was not his, but his brother's wife, Mary Sumner, who founded the Mothers' Union.

CHARLES THOMAS LONGLEY
1. Richmond
   oil
   56½ x 44 ins.
   signed and dated 1862

Archbishop (1862)
In 1867 bishops of the Anglican Communion met together at Lambet in the Guard Room for the first Lambeth Conference. Seventy-six assembled and there was clear differences between High Church an Evangelicals. The result of the Conference was to enhance the statu of the Archbishop's office, and to extend the range of his interests and responsibilities, without increasing h legal jurisdiction.

ARCHIBALD CAMPBELL TAIT
1. Richmond
   Drawing in chalk for oil painting
2. Richmond
   oil
   43 x 28 ins.
   (at London House)
   signed and dated 1879
3. Large oil
   90 x 57 ins.

Archbishop (1869)
The first Scot to be Archbishop of Canterbury. At the age of 31 he succeeded the famous Dr. Arnold as headmaster of Rugby but ill health forced him to leave this work for the Deanery of Carlisle. Tragedy struck on the domestic front and five of his six daughters died within a few week of scarlet fever. The large portrait (hanging out of sequence) shows him as Bishop of London. Sadness struck again with the death of his only son and his devoted wife.

DWARD WHITE ENSON
Ierkomer
5½ x 43 ins.
gned and dated
890

Archbishop (1883)
A man of rare gifts and charm with a power of making lives more vivid. His deepest desire for the Church of England was the renewal of her inner vitality. He sat at Lambeth with five bishops and gave judgment at the famous trial of Bishop King of Lincoln. One of his sons was the writer E. F. Benson, and another became a Monsignor in the Catholic archdiocese of Westminster.

REDERICK EMPLE
Ierkomer
5½ x 43 ins.
igned H. H.

Archbishop (1896)
An ex-headmaster of Rugby, he was always to have an interest in educational reform. An article on Education in the controversial *Essays and Reviews* dogged his career for a while. A Liberal, he also supported the temperance movement. Married at the age of fifty-five, he had sons, and when he moved to Lambeth he improved the plumbing of the Palace, reconstructed the Old Palace at Canterbury, and gave part of the Palace grounds to Lambeth for what is now known as Archbishop's Park. At the age of eighty-one he officiated at Queen Victoria's funeral and crowned Edward VII.

ANDALL THOMAS AVIDSON
. Sargent
32 x 42 ins.
signed and dated
John S. Sargent
1910
. Frank Salisbury
Oil
69 x 41 ins.

Archbishop (1903)
Davidson had been Chaplain to Archbishop Tait and had married his daughter, Edith, in the Chapel at Lambeth. Later as Dean of Windsor he was to become a favourite of Queen Victoria. An able speaker and, owing to Temple's age, much involved in the Coronation of Edward VII, he was well qualified to succeed him. He instituted the Lambeth Diploma, which gives a licence to teach Theology, and which are now conferred each year in the Chapel. At the age of eighty he asked George V if he might retire, and was to be the first Primate to do so. He was made Lord Davidson of Lambeth, and the monument in the centre of the inner courtyard was erected by his friends in his honour.

OSMO GORDON ANG
. de Laszlo
60¼ x 43½ ins.
signed
. Sir William Orpen
49½ x 39 ins. *

Archbishop (1929)
Another Scot, he was a complex and brilliant man. This was the time of the Abdication and Lang was a great Royalist. It was a difficult time for him and he was criticised for his part in its conclusion. In his private diary he wrote 'My heart aches for the Duke of Windsor . . . I cannot bear to think of the kind of life into which he has passed'. He was at Lambeth at the beginning of the war and during the early bombing raids. He resigned in 1942 to make way for a younger man with a fresh approach.

WILLIAM TEMPLE
1. De Laszlo
60 x 42½ ins.
signed and dated
1934
2. Dugdale
35 x 29 ins.
signed

Archbishop (1942)
The son of Frederick Temple, he was much influenced by his father. A brilliant and saintly man, during his brief two and a half years at Lambeth he invested the office of Archbishop of Canterbury as a force to be reckoned with in the land. His early death was a tragedy for the Church of England. These two portraits were painted before he became Archbishop, and show him as a younger man.

GEOFFREY FISHER
Middleton-Todd
50 x 40 ins.
signed and dated 1953

Archbishop (1946)
Another headmaster, Fisher had been at Repton and was known as an excellent organiser. He arrived at Lambeth when much of it was in ruins, and saw the restoration undertaken by the Church Commissioners when they took over responsibility for the Palace. Fisher was to crown Elizabeth II, and to chair the first Assembly of the World Council of Churches and in 1960 made history when he visited Pope John XXIII in Rome.

MICHAEL RAMSEY
George Bruce
57¾ x 42¾ ins.
signed and dated 1982

Archbishop (1961)
Ramsey became the 100th Archbishop of Canterbury on June 27th, 1961. A learned and saintly man, his appearance suggested that he was much older than his years.

(FREDERICK) DONALD COGGAN
William Edward Narraway
49¾ x 39½ ins.
signed and dated 1976

Archbishop (1974)
During Coggan's archiepiscopate the *New English Bible* and *New Testament* was published, and the new alternative services derived their legal status from the Worship and Doctrine Measure 1975.

ROBERT ALEXANDER KENNEDY RUNCIE
David Poole
59½ x 39½ ins.
signed and dated 1987

Archbishop (1980)
The first Archbishop since the Middle Ages to have served as a soldier, when he won the MC. Known for his ecumenism, Dr. Runcie has travelled more widely than his predecessors round the Anglican Communion, and is outspoken on social matters, such as the plight of the Inner Cities. In 1982, when Pope Paul II visited England, Dr. Runcie and the Pope walked side by side up the great aisle of Canterbury Cathedral, and prayed together at the tomb of Thomas a Becket. A truly historical moment.

SLAYERS OF THOMAS A BECKET
British School
15¼ x 9¼ ins.
panel

This was a gift in 1908 and an inscription on the back reads: 'Raynald FitzUrse, Hugh Morrile, Thomas Tracy. Gift 1908 Richard Britton (water-colour) 31.12.1172'

SIR ROBERT WALPOLE
J. B. Van Loo
A version of the portrait at Gatchina, Russia
89 x 58 ins.

Statesman

PETER III IGNATIUS

Syrian Orthodox Patriarch of Antioch (1872–1896)
Visited London in 1874/5 as a guest of Tait. Queen Victoria met him and said 'Now I know what Abraham looked like'.

ABD-ALLAH II

Syrian Orthodox Patriarch 1906–16
Visited London with Peter III and again in 1888 as Benson's guest. Was a great expert on steam engines.

THE FOUR LATIN FATHERS
Flemish School?
55 x 37½ ins.

This picture featured in the trial of Laud and his ownership of it was proof in the eyes of his persecutors that he had Popish tendencies. Laud denied this and claimed that he had inherited it when he came to Lambeth, and it is probable that it came over with Cardinal Pole. The Dove of the Holy Spirit shows signs of being damaged at some period.

GEORGE BERKELEY
British School
50 x 40 ins.

Bishop of Cloyne, 1722

GEORGE HARDING
After Nathaniel Dance
50 x 40 ins.

1766–1816
Author, editor and judge.

Dr. R BYNG
C. Jansen 1648
40¾ x 33¼ ins.

Inscribed Aetatis 67, 1648. Label on back: 'Dr. Rob. Byng of the Palace, Wrotham by C. Jansen 1648'.

ST. DUNSTAN
British School
12 x 8 ins.

With 'The Templer' perched upon his crozier.

KATHARINE PARR
British School
20¾ x 16¾ ins.

The sixth and last wife of Henry VIII.

KING CHARLES I
After Van Dyke
75 x 45 ins.

Supposed to have been given to Laud by Charles I himself.

PRINCE HENRY
After Van Dyke
75 x 45 ins.

This was the Prince of Wales, brother to Charles I, who was a great favourite with the people. He died of cholera.

CANTERBURY CATHEDRAL
Thomas Johnson of Canterbury
58 x 69½ ins.

The south side of the Cathedral showing the building before the tower was built. This used to hang in the Old Palace at Croydon.

MAN WITH FUR COLLAR
British School
26 x 20 ins.

Nothing is known about this picture, other than it dates from the 16th century.

LAMBETH PALACE FROM THE THAMES
W. H. Miller
7¾ x 9¼ ins.

The view from Millbank in the earl
19th century.

BISHOP'S WALK, LAMBETH
Daniel Turner
13¼ x 11¾ ins.
panel

A delightful view of the area befor the Embankment took place. Turne lived at Lambeth, and was better known for his watercolours.

WILLIAM EWART GLADSTONE
C. H. Thompson
40 x 32 ins.

The famous Statesman. Given to Lambeth Palace in 1925 by Mr. Henry Gladstone.

LADY DAVIDSON
De Laszlo
signed and dated 1926
30 x 20½ ins. *

Edith, daughter of Archbishop Tait, and Randall Davidson, his Chaplain married in 1878 and spent 25 years a Lambeth. A silver gilt rose bowl wa given to them on their 50th weddi anniversary by George V, and is on of the treasures at Lambeth.

Mrs. FRANCES TEMPLE
De Laszlo
signed and dated 1934
15¾ x 19½ ins. *

Wife of William Temple, who died i office, Frances Temple outlived he husband by forty years. The portra is inscribed by the artist 'In memo of happy days at Bishopthorpe'.

LADY FISHER
Phillips
90 x 28 ins.
signed *

The mother of six sons, Lady Fish took an active part in church organisations, especially the Mothe Union.

LADY COGGAN
Muriel C. Smith
pastel
27 x 20½ ins.
signed and dated 1963

Lady Coggan was also active in church organisations, and she had a studio at Lambeth where she painted.

VIEW OF MORTON'S TOWER
British School
30 x 50 ins.

Showing the Tower in the 18th cent before the Embankment of the riv Note that the artist has left out a window in the right-hand tower, wh must have been his mistake.

CANTERBURY CATHEDRAL CRYPT
S. Prout
14 x 19½ ins.
bury at Lambeth

Inscribed on the back 'Sketch mad by my father, S. Prout, about the year 1813. To be sent at my death His Grace the Archbishop of Cant bury at Lambeth Palace. S. G. Pro

PORTRAIT OF A LADY WITH RED/GOLD HAIR
British School
27½ x 19 ins.

Until recently this was said to be Penelope, Lady Rich, Countess of Devonshire. Sir Philip Sidney was love with her and dedicated many his sonnets to her. However, the s of her dress is of a later period, an is more likely to be a likeness of a younger member of the Cavendish family.

OLD PALACE, CANTERBURY
W. D. Caroe, Architect
50 x 44 ins.

The architects birds-eye view of t Old Palace, after the reconstructic work he did at the end of the 19t century.